THE FUTURE OF WOMEN WEAR

RETAILING

A Step-by-Step Guide to Discover Profitable Strategies for Indian Women Apparel Retailers

THE FUTURE OF WOMEN WEAR

RETAILING

A Step-by-Step Guide to Discover Profitable Strategies for Indian Women Apparel Retailers

Naveen N Banura
THE SAM WALTON OF APPAREL RETAILING

Worldwide Publishing by
Pendown Press

PENDOWN PRESS
An ISO 9001 & ISO 14001 Certified Co.,
Regd. Office: 2525/193, 1st Floor, Onkar Nagar-A,
Tri Nagar, Delhi-110035
Ph.: 09350849407, 09312235086
E-mail: info@pendownpress.com
Branch Office: 1A/2A, 20, Hari Sadan, Ansari Road,
Daryaganj, New Delhi–110002
Ph.: 011-45794768
Website: PendownPress.com

First Edition: 2022

ISBN: 978-93-5554-152-9

Layout and Cover Designed by Pendown Graphics Team
Printed and Bound in India by Thomson Press India Ltd.

To all my fellow
Business Owners who
Love Apparel Retailing
and
Love Fashion

This book is dedicated
to You!

Contents

Preface i

About Me ii

Why I Am Writing This Book? v

What This Book Will Give You? vi

Acknowledgement vii

Chapter 1   Disruption Is On Its Way 1

Chapter 2   Customers Not Repeating 3

Chapter 3   Customers Not Buying 6

Chapter 4   Competition With Online Sellers 8

Chapter 5   New Customers Not Approaching 9

Chapter 6   Profits Shrinking, Save Your Hard Money From Dead Stock 10

Chapter 7   Do Not Know What And When Customer Will Buy 12

Chapter 8   You Are Not Getting The Best Products 14

Chapter 9   Competitors Are Eating The Market Share ...16

Chapter 10 5 Mistakes Retailers Need To Avoid While Buying? 18

Chapter 11 How To Make Your Designs Fast Selling 20

Chapter 12 Staff Not Supporting 22

Chapter 13 Mindset, Goals, Belief Not Aligned 24

Tips 25

Recap! 27

Choices 28

What To Do Next 29

Preface

Do you want to know the future of Indian Ethnic Women Wear retailing in the next 5 or 10 years?

Are you struggling with shrinking profits?

Is your business not scaling up?

Are you unable to get your children into your business?

Credentials

Heartfelt gratitude to Akshar Sir for unconditional and never-ending support in inspiring me to compile my knowledge and experience into this book to help other entrepreneurs grow.

Love you Always.

About Me

Hello, My Name is Naveen Nagarmal Banura, and I live in the heart of Jaipur, also famously known as the Pink City in Rajasthan - India.

My passion is to create a beautiful community of Retailers where everyone has a flourishing business. Being in this industry for more than 20 years. Currently, I am the Managing Director at M.N. Fashions (India's # 1 Brand in B2B Indian Women Ethnic Wear). In the last 5 years, I have supported over 5000 Retailers to achieve profits crossing 144 crores & saved 55 crores of dead stock.

In my journey of entrepreneurship, I am known as a Retailing Strategist & Expert for Women's Ethnic Wear, creator of the VFC framework and "Icon of Ethnic Garment Industry" Awardee.

If you are wondering why I am making an effort to write a book and share my knowledge and expertise, well, the answer is simple.

I am writing this book because I want to give back to society. It's my payback time. I am thankful to my team, clients, buyers, suppliers, and associates for their never-ending support, care, respect and, for helping me earn a name in the Indian Women's Ethnic Wear industry and for referring me confidently to others.

I promise after reading this book, your business will change radically and grow 10X. It will be a lot of fun and happiness, and you will be living the life you always dreamed of if you just implement what has been shared in this book.

My Mission is to make the Indian Women's Apparel Industry the most profitable and scalable. Also, I wish to upgrade at least 1 lakh Retailers in the process.

21 years ago, when I started my career in Women's Ethnic Wear. I was passionate and was a leading wholesaler for 5–6 years, and then I failed miserably. I learned from my mistakes and never lost hope as I believed that something better was going to happen now. I fought like a warrior and stood my ground throughout the challenging period.

After long research, study, reading many books, attending seminars and workshops and putting in a lot of money, time and effort. I created a FRAMEWORK for Retailers.

I finally decided to compile all my learnings and experience into a book so that many others can learn and achieve the life they want to live.

If you are in this industry and not adapting to the latest changes. You will suffer 100% loss, and revival will be tough.

This is the main reason why apparel retail businesses shut down, and hence no wonder the next generation is not joining your business and taking the legacy forward.

Let's deep dive.

Now, I challenge you to recognise the opportunity that is in your hands. Don't just read this book; pay the price to really become a successful Retailer. Just imagine what would happen to your world of business if your prospects saw you as The Authority. Everybody wants to buy from the best; this book in your hands is a method to crack the code and become the best in the world.

Believe me. You Can Do This!

A well-planned retailing strategy can work wonders for your business irrespective of the apparel retailing you work with, provided it is put together in a seamless and cohesive manner. Trust me; my experience is talking.

Why I Am Writing This Book?

My vision is to help and guide Indian Women Ethnic Wear Retailers to enrich their lives so they can live happily, saving their time to enable them to enjoy their life.

When I see Retailers stuck, struggling for their growth or failing, it breaks my heart to see how Retailers are not growing their business, So I want to extend my help by putting maximum Retailers on the right path. I have already helped more than 1000 Retailers to come out of such situations.

Now I decided to spread my learning and expertise to more and more Retailers.

I believe in "Share your knowledge – So someone gets benefited" if you're not doing this, you are being unfair to others.

That is why I am writing this book to spread my learning and expertise far and wide.

What This Book Will Give You?

You will achieve massive success and revenue if you implement the strategies shared in this book.

In this book, you will learn some interesting and simple hacks to make your Customers happy and grow your business exponentially.

After interacting with more than 1000 Retailers, I understood their pain points and created a framework of solutions. This framework is result-oriented and has already benefited 300+ Retailers.

This book is summarised in 13 beautiful lessons that I have learnt during my journey in the Indian Women's Ethnic Wear Business.

Many of you may know these or perhaps even more than what is written here. This book will help you recall all your knowledge and bring in the change in a smooth manner.

I am sure these lessons will steer you to the path of success in Retailing Business. So, without further ado, let's explore the 13 lessons and tips.

Your friendly Women Apparel Retailing Strategist.

– Naveen N Banura

Acknowledgement

First and foremost, I would like to thank my parents, who gave me abundant love and provided a nurturing environment during my early childhood years, which enabled me to grow up as a confident, independent person.

I would also like to extend my appreciation to all my buyers for their valuable suggestions, feedback, and encouragement to publish a book that could be helpful for everyone.

Chapter 1

Disruption Is On Its Way

The Women's apparel market was projected to reach nearly 39 billion USD by 2025 in India, a significant increase since 2015. The rise in the working Women population in India projected this growth in the apparel market over the next decade, among other reasons. Ethnic Wear had the largest market value within the sector. According to a survey, Festivals and special occasions were the primary reasons for Ethnic Wear purchase among Indians. (Published by Statista Research Department, Nov. 10, 2021)

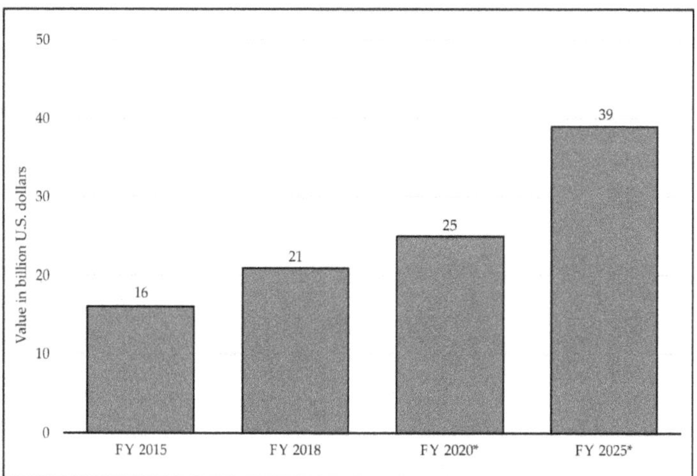

Now, Market demand is changing in a radical way. Women's first choice is instant Ready to Wear Garments.

The industry is in disruption. As a Retailer, you have to upgrade and upscale for the future in readymade Wear.

Those who have already adapted to this ecosystem are starting to keep pace with the market, and for those who are still thinking, I advise you to START. It's time to upgrade; start selling Readymade Wear in your retail shop.

Chapter 2

Customers Not Repeating

*"People do not buy goods & services.
They buy relations, stories & magic".*

– Seth Godin

You can grow your business exponentially even with existing Customers in an easy and effective way because they know you better. Use this to your advantage, and make Customers buy from you repeatedly.

- Let your Customers talk about you. Make them your brand ambassadors.

- Integrity in your dealings and transactions with Customers is the best thing. Do the right things even when nobody's watching!

- Create extra value for them by knowing their desire.

- Make a brand and put all your power into making it famous.

- You have to care and show them your intent.

- Customer Delight must be your priority.

- Focus on relationship building first.

- Target the right Customers. Identify your right Customers first.

- Create a value system; Customer connect is the essential key.

- Maintain a database of Customers. Informative messages or greetings, or any launch news will help you to stay connected.

- Ask Customers for reviews and feedback. Make a call to Customers after purchase and ask if they are happy with their outfit.

- Connect with Customers through emotions.

- You must have a strong base which builds trust in the Customer's mind, like a clean and properly managed outlet.

- Be flexible with your Customer.

- Have a fixed price policy or equal pricing for all to build trust in the Customer's mind.

- Try to identify and understand the buying pattern of your Customers.

- Greet your Customers on their birthdays and anniversaries.

Let me share with you the pattern a store in Delhi uses after following my strategy.

Whenever a famous, big, reputed school has a Parents Teacher Meet, the store communicates with existing Customers (especially mothers of the kids going to that school) and shares new arrivals of dresses ideal for the PTM. As a result, the store gets quick sales from existing Customers.

Chapter 3

Customers Not Buying

- Without a strong why people don't buy.

- Hick's Law (or the Hick-Hyman Law) states that the more stimuli (or choices) users face, the longer it will take them to make a decision.

- Your Customer is initially attracted to a wide variety, but when making a purchase decision with more choice, the decision-making process freezes.

- It's always better to ask for specific choices and show fewer but relevant designs.

- More designs will only end up distracting them.

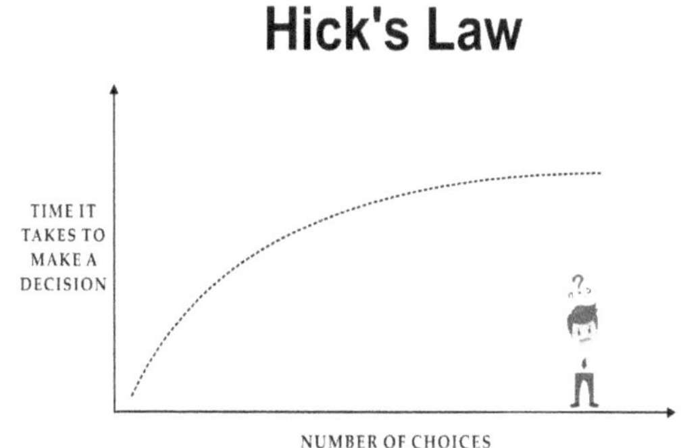

Let me share with you something, one of my buyers based in Mumbai was facing this issue. Many times Customers were not buying despite having a strong requirement. The Customer was taking a long time to finalise or visited 2–3 times to finalise the same dress and many times ended up never even buying. When he discussed the problem with me, I shared the focused strategy of showing products as per the Customer's requirement only. Then we designed and created a framework of questions to know and understand more about the Customer's needs.

Now in his showroom, they have a rule of asking for the purpose of buying the particular dress, colour, style, and imagination in the Customer Customer's mind. After all these, the staff shows 5–8 dresses only and 93% of Customers buy from the products shown. Train your staff to understand requirements in a decent way.

So Do Not Sell, Let Customers Buy From You.

Chapter 4

Competition With Online Sellers

These days I see many Retailers are afraid of online sellers. You never have to let this fear overpower your mind. You and your store are far better than online sellers. Most Online sellers are not selling what they are showing.

Be confident and calm, and focus on your target Customers.

Also, you can reach your Customers through pre-scheduled video calls, WhatsApp sharing and other ways if they are not inclined to visit the store always.

You have the power of your experience, and you have products in stock. Offer a much more delightful and personalised buying experience to your Customers.

Preference to wear and try before purchase, store image and brand loyalty.

All this makes your brand and showroom more powerful as compared to online sellers.

Chapter 5

New Customers Not Approaching

Gone are the days when a Retailer waited for Customers to walk into their stores. Today the scenario is totally different. Actually, you have to approach new Customers. Let Customers come to know about your brand and showroom

Share testimonials and happy client reviews on social media, in your ads, blogs, and website.

Testimonials are like snipper tools.

Pick any one social media handle like YouTube or Telegram channels and post informative content and videos frequently to help Customers buy the right products.

Ask Existing Customers for referrals. This works great.

Sponsor local events and programs in your area from time to time, so new Customers can know about your store and products.

Take help from influencers on social media to promote your product and brand.

Chapter 6

Profits Shrinking, Save Your Hard Money From Dead Stock

This is the most important and crucial part of the book.

Here are some bullets to capture this in an easy way.

1. Buy in small portions but with more billing cycles so that you always get the latest stock.

2. Focus on products which are rocket selling. Keep continuing with those hit products.

3. Always purchase precisely. Do not come under pressure from suppliers like minimum buying of this amount is required or such.

4. Buy from B2B suppliers and wholesalers who have filtered collections from which you will choose. So, you get the best.

5. Always focus on original and quality products, and keep yourself away from copied products.

6. Review, in 15 days, the Total Purchased Garments and Total Sold Garments of a particular supplier to

get a clear picture of all suppliers and how their products are performing at your store.

7. Analyse and review your expenses monthly. Believe me, just by analysing alone; you can save up to 20% of the amount you are spending.

8. Get in touch with your Supplier for insights on how to save more money.

Improve your retailing strategies to increase your retail sales by offering well-maintained retail services, facilities, promotions and quality merchandise.

Chapter 7

Do Not Know What
And When Customer Will Buy

Always associate with the number 1 supplier or big Suppliers having the best infrastructure, strong foundation, and system-driven technology to get insights into the upcoming market and fashion trends from time to time.

It is very important for you to stay updated by being in touch with market trends and being well-informed about what is happening. You must know what garment styles are in fashion or will be trending. This is what your client wants from you.

Recent research studies show different buying habits in Fig 1.

Like In India, Women's Ethnic Wear consumers are more inclined than consumers in other markets to buy apparel for a specific purpose. Indeed, 38 per cent of Indian respondents to a recent McKinsey study said they were highly likely to buy apparel for special events, a significantly higher proportion as compared to Brazil (5%), Russia (3%) or China! (6%).

<table>
<tr><td>

A. Do you buy Branded apparels

3%

97%

Yes No

</td><td>

B. Which brands do u prefer to buy

40% 35%

25%

National International A combination of both

</td></tr>
<tr><td>

C. Where do yo prefer to go for shopping

10%

22%

68%

Malls Traditional shops E-shopping

</td><td>

D. Do you buy clothing for special events such as weddings, festivals, parties

11%

89%

Yes No

</td></tr>
<tr><td>

E. How frequently you buy branded apparel

10%

60% 30%

Weekly Monthly Occassionally

</td><td>

F. Average spending on branded apparel on every shopping visit

10% 25%

20%

45%

Less than 3000   3000-6000

6000-9000   9000-12000 and above

</td></tr>
</table>

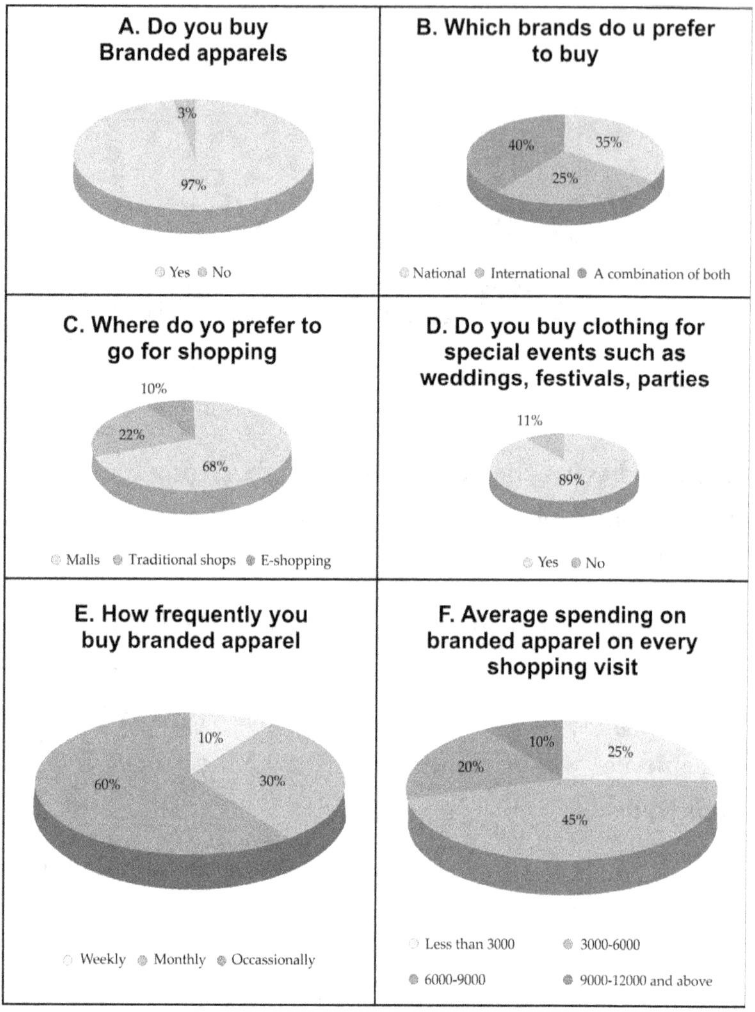

Chapter 8

You Are Not Getting
The Best Products

Always associate with the best Supplier in the industry.

A good Supplier will always guide you on which styles you must focus on.

Rocket Selling Designs must be a part of your collection.

These are like magnets that attract Customers and force them to refer you to others.

Make sure you are on the top buyer list of your Supplier.

Suppliers always take care of their premium buyers.

Be their premium buyer.

Make payments as per the agreed terms before your Supplier asks.

Stay connected with your Supplier, and keep in touch.

Share feedback, advice, and forecasting with the Supplier and show your skills.

Always buy in small segments to maintain flow and payment routine.

Discuss your genuine problems with your Suppliers as they are your support system.

Believe me; you can only grow together when a strong bonding between you and your Supplier is established and lasts forever.

Once you support your Supplier, they will open their heart to you.

Do work with those suppliers whose intent is "*Grahak hi Bhagwan hai*".

Chapter 9

Competitors Are Eating
The Market Share

You must have a strong reason; find your why (why here refers to your purpose, you should find your purpose for starting that business).

Selling goods/products to the Customers through manipulative tactics or fear is a short-term tool/strategy with short-term results.

"People don't buy WHAT you do; they buy WHY you do it."

Apple's ability to command fierce loyalty for its truly innovative products goes beyond WHAT they do into WHY they do it. iPod was not the first mp3 player in the market (Singapore-based Creative Technologies was the pioneer).

However, it soon became the category leader while earning heavy margins. Creative sold its mp3 players with "5 G.B. capacity" (WHAT), while Apple sold its iPod with "100 songs in your pocket" (WHY).

Apple integrated its iPod with iTunes and allowed users to download a single track instead of an entire album, thereby giving more "WHY" reasons to buy.

Don't worry about the competition. Actually, other stores are helping you so your Customer can judge, compare others and choose you over them.

Keep your products innovative, show Customers what they want, and satisfy their desires. Your Customers will stay with you forever and also refer you to others.

Chapter 10

5 Mistakes Retailers Need To Avoid While Buying?

1. **Ignoring fit standards.**

   Never ever ignore the quality of the fit of the products you are purchasing. This will save you huge time on alteration. Proper fitting in the first trial means more happy Customers. Follow the universal standard fit guidelines to maintain the quality of fitting

2. **Lack of knowledge of fabric gradation used in the garment.**

   Ask for the fabric details or standards/ parameters the suppliers used to manufacture the garments.

3. **Buying in bulk after long intervals.**

   A very common mistake Retailers make to avoid travel is they buy in bulk. Find the right Supplier who has the system to update you about new launches and can deliver at your doorstep at your convenience.

4. **Buying low-quality copy items.**

   Always buy original products with the best quality fabric and stitching and workmanship parameters used. Ask for any lab certifications like Liva or Nissenken. Certifications give a guarantee of quality. This creates an impact on your clientele and builds trust in your brand.

5. **Never ask for a photo shoot or video with their brand.**

   Always ask for a Model Shoot of garments if the Supplier has them, so you can save your cost on shoots and boost your sales by using these on Social Media with your brand logo.

Always take care of the above points to make your collection the best and unique.

Chapter 11

How To Make
Your Designs Fast Selling

*"Identify your problems,
but give your power and energy to solutions."*

BRANDING IS EVERYTHING

See the above picture, you will understand the power of branding. All you have to do is focus on it. Create your brand to ensure Customers can talk about it

Relate your products with the trends going on in the fashion industry.

Show your Customers fashion magazines, blogs, and print articles, so Customers can take the right buying decision.

Display Model Shoot Videos and Photos on a Big Screen where Customers can easily see your designs. This helps them to buy quickly.

Use the principle of displaying your product from left to right because the human eye sees the left first and then travels to the right.

Make loud noise on social media platforms like Instagram, Facebook and others. You better know and believe that "*Jo Dikhta Hai Woh Bikta Hai*", meaning that which is visible, sells and create the brand.

Chapter 12

Staff Not Supporting

Always keep Josh (passion) high in your team. Always appreciate them in front of everyone. If they need to be scolded for something, do it in private.

Involve your staff in your growth. Show them the path and ask for suggestions. What do they feel or want for the growth of the brand?

Instead of verbally delegating work, try to delegate tasks in writing.

Create your brand image and make your entire staff look consistent as representatives of your brand. Get uniformity by giving specially designed uniforms for them, preferably showcasing your brand colors.

Failing to give proper recognition

The most basic form of disrespect is not giving proper recognition for a job well done. So, celebrate the small wins they bring for the brand.

Create a system for awarding or recognising your top performers.

Start every day fresh. Play some spiritual music in the showroom, and perform daily prayers. Learn the art of appreciation, expressing gratitude and affirmations. Train your team as well.

Connect emotionally with your team. Create bonds with your team. They spend approximately 33% of their time daily on your growth.

Failing to express gratitude

Saying thank you doesn't cost anything and motivates the team members – Owners often have a difficult time expressing gratitude.

Make your place a great place to work so more staff have a desire to join you. Create a healthy, fun environment at work.

Celebrations always bring in prosperity. Treat your team twice annually, and once, you may invite their family on a special occasion.

Create systems and ensure you follow them for your and your team's growth.

Sometimes, after all your best efforts, if some staff is not performing, it's better to say goodbye to them.

Chapter 13

Mindset, Goals, Beliefs

"Where focus goes, energy flows."

You become rich in your mind long before you become rich in your bank account.

It is all a game of mindset. I am writing about this because your belief system, goals and mindset are going to transform your life 360 degrees.

Write your Goals for business, personal life, family and your intellectual desires. Review and update these goals frequently. Plan and take action strategically to achieve these goals.

Beliefs are going to impact your life in a massive way; you know, "Thought Becomes Reality".

Watch movies on manifestation like The Secret and The Peaceful Warrior.

Tips

I am sharing what I do and recommend you to do so too.

These are some of the tips I am following, and I suggest you try following them and see the difference:

1. Read good books. These are your silent motivators.
2. Keep yourself healthy. A healthy body has a healthy mindset.
3. Keep scheduling your day, week, month, and year.
4. Spend more time with your family. It charges you up.
5. Take a break, and enjoy the holiday.
6. Set your goal and plan for it. A goal without a plan is just a wish.
7. Be grateful for what you have. You have to give more to receive more.
8. Always have a positive mindset.
9. Never do multiple things at the same time. Do one thing at a time.
10. "Every problem is a gift--without problems, we would not grow."

11. If you do what you've always done, you'll get what you've always got."

12. Improve yourself and your business by 1% every day, and you'll notice that both of you are 37 times better by the end of the year. Small steps bring big results.

13. Focus on becoming a Trusted Retail Showroom.

Recap!

"Life is always Happening for us, not to us".

–Tony Robbins

So, this is the whole content of the book. To Sum up, I would say, be prepared for the future. There is immense scope in the Women's Ethnic Wear business. *"Jarurat hai apne aap ko upscale karne ki, tayar karneki, aane wala kal aaj se bahut behtar hai."*

Try to implement one point at a time to see its effective results and then move to the other points.

Choices

Think about what you want to do- You have two choices.

Either you can do it all by yourself. You may be successful, or you may not be.

OR

If you are looking for sure shot results in a limited time span, Schedule a meeting with me right away. I will help you to achieve 10 x growth and become the best retail showroom in 5 months

Write to me now at nb@mnfashions.com.

I will personally take out time to serve you.

What To Do Next

1. Connect with me on LinkedIn www.linkedin.com/in/naveenbanura

2. Schedule your appointment at M.N. Fashions to grow your business. www.calendly.com/mnfashions/visitor